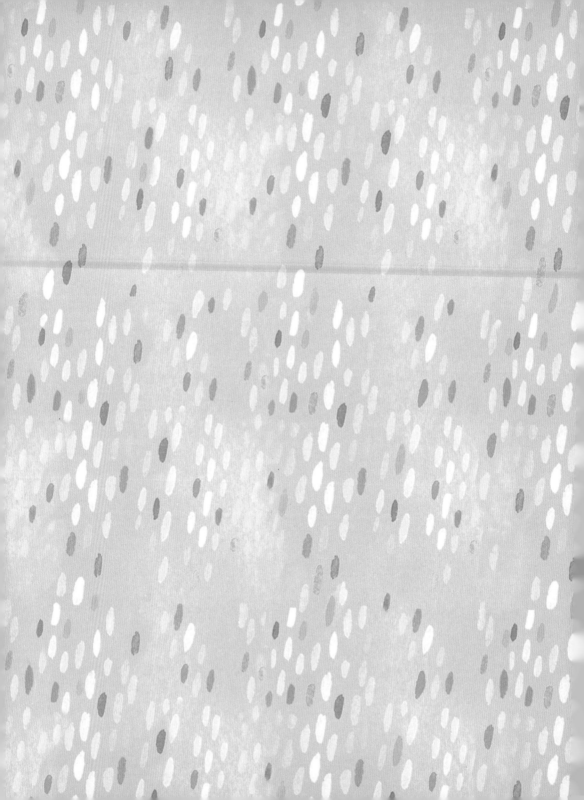

A Gift For:

Delilah

From:

Grandma
Christmas 2016

Editorial Director: Carrie Bolin
Art Director: Chris Opheim
Designer: Laura Elsenraat
Production Designer: Dan Horton

ISBN: 978-1-59530-790-3
BOK1046

Made in China
NOV15

THE FAIRIES' GUIDE
to Taking Life Lightly

BY STACEY DONOVAN

Hallmark

Make today your chance...
to dream a new dream...
to notice something beautiful...
to do something silly...
to really listen to someone...
to be happiness.

Go ahead and twirl
when no one else
is looking...
or even better,
when they are.

Just like bees gather nectar
from every flower,
gather little moments
here and there
to make your life sweet.

Dream big.

Or dream medium.

 Little dreams are fine, too.

JUST DREAM.

Don't be afraid to sparkle...

Someone else may need your light.

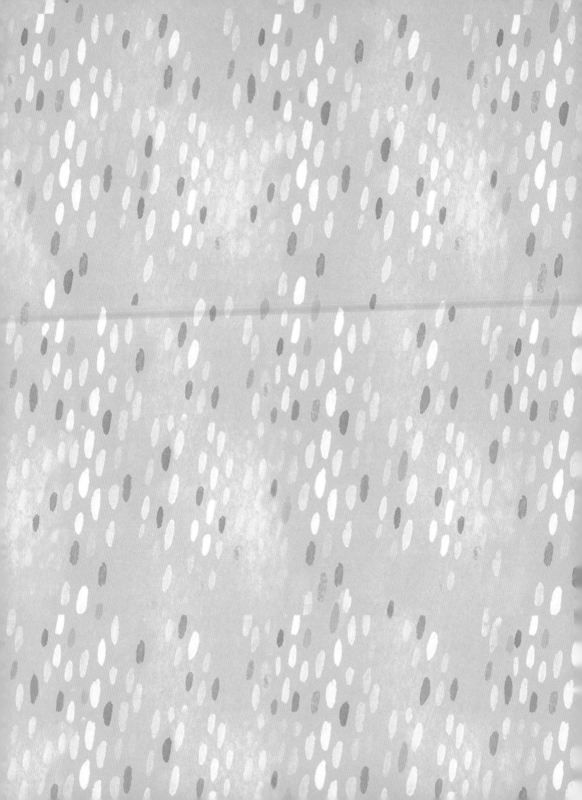

Take a nice, deep breath.
Hey, take two. THEY'RE FREE.

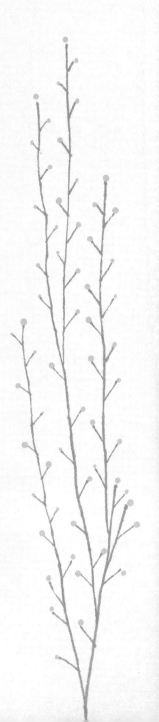

If you could see in your reflection

all the wonderful things other people see in you,

you would never stop staring at yourself.

Take today by the hand
and skip out into the sunshine.

Be like a bird and keep on singing.

Make like a cricket and keep on chirping.

Be happy in the way

that only you can do.

Positive thoughts
make colors brighter...
stars sparklier...
everything better.

The **KINDNESS** you give away all day

will give you *SWEET DREAMS* at night.

Put off all your worrying until tomorrow...

And do the same thing tomorrow, too.

Believe in yourself
and, no matter what,
you have one person
on your side.

DO ONE NEW THING TODAY...

take a new way home,
listen to a new song,
wear a different color...

Because new things
can refresh your soul
like rain on a thirsty flower.

Every forest has many paths...
It's never too late to try out another one.

TAKE A LEAP

because you were born to fly!

Sometimes we find
smiles in the most unlikely places
and friends in the most
unexpected people.

DON'T HOLD ON TO REGRETS...

You have enough to keep track of.

Just because you tripped
that one time doesn't mean
you can't dance.

There's a lot of fun
to be had in this world,
and somebody's got to do it.

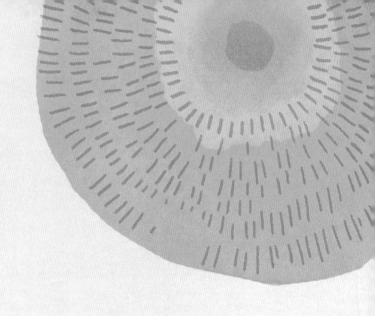

MAY AS WELL BE YOU.

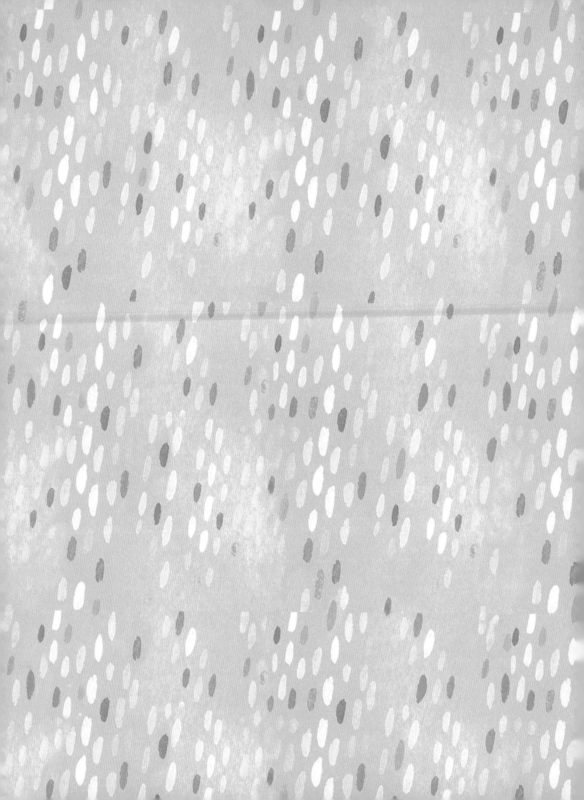

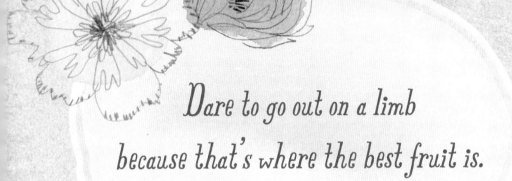

Dare to go out on a limb
because that's where the best fruit is.

Take care of yourself
and it will be easier
to take care of everyone else.

Sometimes, wasting time is the wisest thing you can do.

Enjoy some time to yourself,
because you are excellent company.

Let the rain *kiss your skin*.

Let the sun *warm your face*.

Experience every moment...

See what it teaches...

Follow where it leads.

Keep being yourself...
Nobody else can do it!
They wouldn't even be
good at it if they tried.

IMAGINE

tossing your worries

like leaves into a stream

and watching them

drift, drift away.

Do something you once LOVED doing...

DRAW (or paint) (or color)

RUN

watch clouds

PICK FLOWERS

blow soap bubbles

And see if it still brings you
that same sense of magic.

(BET IT WILL!)

HERE COMES JOY

and all you have to do
is hold out your hands.

Go ahead
and hand out encouragement
like everybody needs it...

because they do.

No one else remembers
the little mistakes
you've made,
so why should you?

The world is full of people
who haven't met you yet,
and they are just going
to love you.

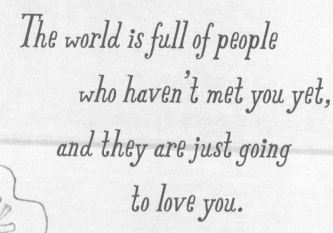

Make a wish on every
star you can find
in the sky.

Why limit yourself to just one?

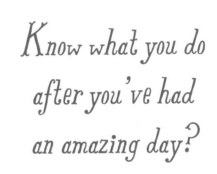

Know what you do
after you've had
an amazing day?

GO OUT AND DO IT AGAIN.

If you have enjoyed this book
or it has touched your life in some way,
we would love to hear from you.

PLEASE SEND YOUR COMMENTS TO:
Hallmark Book Feedback
P.O. Box 419034 Mail Drop 100
Kansas City, MO 64141

Or e-mail us at: booknotes@hallmark.com